What Wo You Do?

Moral Dilemmas

BOOK 2

What Would You Do? products available in print or eBook form.

Book 1 • Book 2

Written by
Michael O. Baker

Edited by
Stephanie Stevens
Patricia Gray

Cover Design by
Anna Allshouse

© 2017, 2008, 1989
THE CRITICAL THINKING CO.™
www.CriticalThinking.com
Phone: 800-458-4849 • Fax: 541-756-1758
1991 Sherman Ave., Suite 200 • North Bend • OR 97459
ISBN 978-0-89455-349-3

MIX
Paper from
responsible sources
FSC® C011935

INTRODUCTION

Rationale

The purpose of this book is NOT to teach moral values or ethical standards. These moral dilemmas provide a rich opportunity for students to apply their individual moral values in difficult and complex situations that they will likely encounter sometime in their lives. The discussion problems also improve listening, communication, and critical thinking skills.

Teaching Suggestions

Read an activity aloud or reproduce student copies of a problem (activity). Ask each student to respond only to what he or she would do, not to what someone else has stated.

An alternative teaching method is to ask students to write a response to the initial problem before engaging in any of the subsequent discussion questions. Students are often surprised to learn that what they thought was a simple decision requires careful analysis. Asking a student to make a decision before discussing the problem with peers forces a decision based on his or her own moral beliefs. This also gives the individual a better appreciation of how we differ from each other and sometimes how we can learn from each other's insights.

Asking for more information or clarification is often a sign that a student is carefully analyzing the question. If a student asks for more information before making a decision, be sure to ask why the additional information is wanted.

Some questions ask, "What if the person is disabled?" These are not attempts to lead students to sympathetic or unsympathetic views of disabled people. The purpose is to have students question whether a person's disability would have any bearing on the situation.

PROBLEM 1

> Suppose someone tells you that he or she is envious that you have many friends and, because of this, asks you for help in making friends. Most of your friends, however, think this person is "weird."

1. a. Would you invite this person to take part in some activities with you and your friends?

    b. Would you consider the problem unfortunate but not something that you can solve?

    c. Would you refrain from inviting this person to socialize with your friends but make suggestions about how to make some friends?

    d. Would you do something else? What would you do?

2. What if this person lives next door to you and you see each other all the time? Would this change what you would do? Explain why.

3. What if both sets of parents know each other, and your parents ask you to help this person make some friends? Would this change what you would do? Explain why.

4. What if a few of your friends tell you they do not want this person hanging around with them? Would this change what you would do? Explain why.

5. What if, whenever you spend some time with this person, some of your friends avoid you? Would this change what you would do? Explain why.

6. What if this person begins to follow you around and/or tries to associate with you before you decide what to do? Would this change what you would do? Explain why.

7. What if this person tells you he or she is very lonely? Would this change what you would do? Explain why.

PROBLEM 2

Suppose you are an athlete and are offered a legal, performance-enhancing drug before an athletic competition.

1.
   a. Would you take the drug?

   b. Would you decline the offer of the drug?

   c. Would you talk to your parents or a person in authority about the drug offer?

   d. Would you do something else? What would you do?

2. What if you find out that most of the other people in the competition are using the drug? Would this change what you would do? Explain why.

3. What if none of the other people in the competition are using the drug? Would this change what you would do? Explain why.

4. What if you think that taking the drug will help you win a state championship or a scholarship to college? Would this change what you would do? Explain why.

5. What if there is some concern among medical researchers that the drug may have harmful, long-term effects on your health? Would this change what you would do? Explain why.

6. What if the performance-enhancing drug is not legal? Would this change what you would do? Explain why.

7. What if you find out that most of the other people in the competition are using the illegal drug? Would this change what you would do? Explain why.

8. What if none of the other people in the competition are using the illegal drug? Would this change what you would do? Explain why.

9. What if you think that taking the illegal drug will help you win a state championship and/or a scholarship to college? Would this change what you would do? Explain why.

PROBLEM 3

Suppose you go into a store to buy a few items. After your items are added up, the cashier gives you a total that is about half of what you expected.

1.   a.   Would you ask the cashier if there is a mistake before paying the amount?

   b.   Would you pay the bill and remain silent?

   c.   Would you pay the bill and then comment as you are leaving that the bill is not as much as you expected?

   d.   Would you do something else? What would you do?

2.   What if the cashier is someone you know? Would this change what you would do? Explain why.

3.   What if the cashier seems very sad about something? Would this change what you would do? Explain why.

4.   What if the cashier is not very friendly? Would this change what you would do? Explain why.

5.   What if the prices in the store are higher than those in some other stores around the area? Would this change what you would do? Explain why.

6.   What if you suspect a cashier at the same store charged you too much for a previous purchase? Would this change what you would do? Explain why.

7.   What if the store is not in your town, and you do not plan to return to the area for a long time? Would this change what you would do? Explain why.

8.   What if you know the person who owns the store? Would this change what you would do? Explain why.

9.   What if you have been out of work for six months and don't have a lot of money? Would this change what you would do? Explain why.

10.   What if you are wealthy? Would this change what you would do? Explain why.

PROBLEM 4

Suppose you are a teenage actor or actress living with your parents. You receive a three-year acting contract that pays $300,000 a year. Your parents are middle-income earners. Your parents ask you to share your earnings equally with your brother and sister.

1.
   a. Would you do as your parents ask?
   b. Would you refuse to share your earnings with your brother and sister?
   c. Would you question the fairness of the request?
   d. Would you do something else? What would you do?

2. What if you believe your brother and sister would spend all the money on clothes and recreation and not save any of it? Would this change what you would do? Explain why.

3. What if your brother and sister had been given the opportunity to get involved in acting, but they declined? Would this change what you would do? Explain why.

4. What if your father has a terminal illness and will probably die within five years? Would this change what you would do? Explain why.

5. What if your mother has a terminal illness and will probably die within five years? Would this change what you would do? Explain why.

6. What if your parents ask you to decide the amount of money (if any) you will give our brother and sister? How much would you give each one? Explain why you came up with that amount.

7. What if your brother and sister are not very nice to you, or what if one of them is nicer to you than the other? Would this change what you would do? Explain why.

8. What if your parents want you to give your brother and sister the money to attend college? Would this change what you would do? Explain why.

PROBLEM 5

Suppose you discover that someone you know often disciplines his or her dog by kicking it or whipping it.

1.
   a. Would you consider the situation to be unfortunate but none of your business?

   b. Would you consider this type of discipline to be unfortunate but sometimes justified?

   c. Would you report the owner to an animal welfare organization?

   d. Would you try to convince the owner to treat the dog humanely?

   e. Would you do something else? What would you do?

2. What if the dog is from one of your dog's litters? Would this change what you would do? Explain why.

3. What if the dog never does what the owner tells it to do? Would this change what you would do? Explain why.

4. What if you see the dog limping badly one day? Would this change what you would do? Explain why.

5. What if the person is a friend of yours? Would this change what you would do? Explain why.

6. What if you talk to the owner, and you are told that physical discipline is the only thing the dog understands? Would this change what you would do? Explain why.

PROBLEM 6

Suppose you are walking down the street, and someone approaches you to ask for some spare change.

1.   a.   Would you ignore the person and keep walking?

        b.   Would you give the person some money?

        c.   Would you ask the person what the money will be used for?

        d.   Would you report the person to the police?

        e.   Would you do something else? What would you do?

2.   What if the person is very thin and appears to be underfed? Would this change what you would do? Explain why.

3.   What if the person is very dirty and sleeps on the ground? Would this change what you would do? Explain why.

4.   What if the person is a young girl? Would this change what you would do? Explain why.

5.   What if the person is a young boy? Would this change what you would do? Explain why.

6.   What if the person tells you the money is for charity? Would this change what you would do? Explain why.

7.   What if the person is very old? Would this change what you would do? Explain why.

PROBLEM 7

Suppose you find out that someone has stolen something.

---

1. a. Would you keep the information to yourself?

    b. Would you try to convince the person to return the stolen item?

    c. Would you report the person to the authorities?

    d. Would you do something else? What would you do?

2. What if the item the person stole is worth over five hundred dollars? Would this change what you would do? Explain why.

3. What if the stolen item has little monetary value but has a high sentimental value to its owner (for example, an old photograph)? Would this change what you would do? Explain why.

4. What if the person who stole is a good friend of yours? Would this change what you would do? Explain why.

5. What if the person who stole is a member of your family? Would this change what you would do? Explain why.

6. What if the person stole the item from a church? Would this change what you would do? Explain why.

7. What if the person stole food and comes from a poor family? Would this change what you would do? Explain why.

8. What if the person who stole tells you about it, asks you not to tell, and reminds you that a favor is owed? Would this change your decision? Explain why.

9. What if the person who stole tells you, "The victim did something mean to me a year ago." Would this change what you would do? Explain why.

PROBLEM 8

Suppose your best friend likes to make fun of people. One day you realize that fewer and fewer people like your friend. You tell your friend about the problem, but he or she doesn't seem to care.

1. a. Would you stick by your best friend and ignore the other people?

    b. Would you try to distance yourself from this person and look for a new best friend?

    c. Would you do something else? What would you do?

2. What if some classmates start distancing themselves from you as well as from your friend? Would this change what you would do? Explain why.

3. What if you find out your friend is moving in two months? Would this change what you would do? Explain why.

4. What if you see that the teasing is hurting the feelings of your other friends? Would this change what you would do? Explain why.

5. What if you find out your friend's parents are getting divorced? Would this change what you would do? Explain why.

6. What if your friend has been more critical of you lately but in a joking manner? Would this change what you would do? Explain why.

7. What if your best friend has been your only close friend for the last few years, and no one else seems to like you as much? Would this change what you would do? Explain why.

PROBLEM 9

Suppose someone you consider physically unattractive asks you for a date.

---

1.   a.   Would you decline the date? If so, what would you say?

        b.   Would you accept the date?

        c.   Would you avoid having to say "yes" or "no" by making up an excuse?

        d.   Would you do something else? What would you do?

2.   What if some of your friends think this person is physically attractive? Would this change what you would do? Explain why.

3.   What if all your friends find this person physically unattractive? Would this change what you would do? Explain why.

4.   What if this person asks you to a school event (for example, a basketball game), and tells you that the two of you would go just as friends? Would this change what you would do? Explain why.

5.   What if some of your friends begin to laugh and tease you when they hear this person has asked you for a date? Would this change what you would do? Explain why.

6.   What if you overheard some students teasing the person who asked you out and telling him or her that you would never accept? Would this change what you would do? Explain why.

7.   What if this person is very shy, and this is the first time that he or she has asked anyone out? Would this change what you would do? Explain why.

8.   What if this person asks you to a dance, but you are hoping to ask–or be asked by–someone else? Would this change what you would do? Explain why.

PROBLEM 10

Suppose you are in line in the school cafeteria. There are two main dishes being served: fish and lasagne. You like fish, but lasagne is your favorite food. The person serving the food asks if you would like one or two helpings of lasagne. You are not sure if you can eat more than one helping. You are allowed to have another helping later if there is any left after everyone has been through the line once. There is always plenty of fish left over.

1.   a.   Would you take one helping and hope it will be enough?

        b.   Would you take two helpings?

        c.   Would you do something else? What would you do?

2. What if, from past experience, you know the kitchen always runs out of lasagne before everyone has been through the line once? Would this change what you would do? Explain why.

3. What if the extra helping of lasagne costs you two dollars? Would this change what you would do? Explain why.

4. What if the extra helping of lasagne costs you ten cents? Would this change what you would do? Explain why.

5. What if the cook tells you there is more than enough for everyone? Would this change what you would do? Explain why.

        a.   If the kitchen gives any remaining food to a shelter for homeless people, would this change what you would do? Explain why.

        b.   If the remaining food will be given to the county prison, would this change what you would do? Explain why.

        c.   If the remaining food will be given to local farmers to feed their pigs, would this change what you would do? Explain why.

PROBLEM 11

Suppose you see someone spraying graffiti on a public statue.

1.   a.   Would you consider it none of your business?

           b.   Would you report it to the police?

           c.   Would you feel that because the property is public and does not belong to one particular individual it is not your responsibility?

           d.   Would you do something else? What would you do?

2.   What if, instead of spraying graffiti, the person is destroying the statue with a hammer? Would this change what you would do? Explain why.

3.   What if the public property is a city bus that has already been spray-painted with graffiti? Would this change what you would do? Explain why.

4.   What if the public property is a locker in a public school? Would this change what you would do? Explain why.

5.   What if you see someone throw an empty can into a river? What you would do? Explain why.

6.   What if you see someone litter a public highway with a newspaper? What you would do? Explain why.

7.   What if you see a person litter with a cigarette butt? Would this change what you would do? Explain why.

PROBLEM 12

Suppose you ask your parents if you may have a party. Your parents give their permission but ask you to limit the party to ten people. You have more than ten friends.

1. a. Would you pick ten of your best friends and hope that your other friends (who are not invited) will not feel hurt?

    b. Would you pick ten of your twelve best friends and then ask them not to say anything about the party to anyone who is not invited?

    c. Would you decide not to have a party?

    d. Would you do something else? What would you do?

2. What if you have ten close friends, and four other good friends have invited you to their parties? Would this change what you would do? Explain why.

3. What if, before finding out you could only invite ten people, you already told twenty-one people you were going to have a party? Would this change what you would do? Explain why.

4. What if your parents ask you to limit the party to four people? Would this change what you would do? Explain why.

PROBLEM 13

Suppose you are considering getting married. After each question, decide whether a disagreement with your partner over this question would cause you to postpone or cancel your marriage plans.

1. Would you prefer to have your spouse earning an income? Explain why.

2. If your spouse earns an income, would it bother you if your spouse earned a lot more than you? Explain why.

3. Who should make the decisions involving purchases for your home? Explain why.

4. Who should decide if and when to have children? Explain why.

5. Who should make the decisions involving buying clothes for the children? Explain why.

6. Who should be responsible for cooking dinner? Explain why.

7. Who should be responsible for housework? Explain why.

8. Who should be responsible for yard work? Explain why.

9. In order to keep your job, you must accept a transfer to another city. Who should decide whether you and your partner move so that you can keep your job? Explain why.
   a. What factors would be important to your decision?
   b. What if your spouse would have to change careers if you accept the transfer? Would this change what you would do? Explain why.

10. Who should decide what religious beliefs the children will be raised with? Explain why.

11. If the family has only enough money for one new car and one used car, who should drive each car?
    a. What if your spouse needs the car for sales calls, while you could take a bus to work? Would this change your decision? Explain why.

PROBLEM 14

Suppose you find a nice-looking ring on the floor of a large store in a shopping mall. You estimate the ring's value to be somewhere around four hundred dollars. The ring does not contain any sort of identifying mark or inscription. It is dusty and appears to have been there at least a month or more. The policy of the store is to give all unclaimed items to charity.

---

1. a. Would you turn in the ring to the store's lost and found department?

    b. Would you keep the ring?

    c. Would you do something else? What would you do?

2. What if you ask someone at the lost and found department if anyone has reported losing a ring, and they tell you that no one has reported a lost ring recently? Would this change what you would do? Explain why.

3. What if the person at the lost and found department tells you that someone called two weeks ago asking about a ring which matches the description of the one you found, but he did not leave a phone number or an address and has not called back since? Would this change what you would do? Explain why.

4. What if the ring does not fit any of your fingers? Would this change what you would do? Explain why.

5. What if you think the ring is beautiful? Would this change what you would do? Explain why.

6. What if you think the ring is not very attractive? Would this change what you would do? Explain why.

7. What if you have a friend in the hospital, and you believe the ring might cheer her up? Would this change what you would do? Explain why.

8. What if the policy is to sell all unclaimed items at the end of the year for a profit? Would this change what you would do? Explain why.

PROBLEM 15

Suppose a friend of yours is so overweight that he or she is always the brunt of jokes. You enjoy each other's company, but you fear your friend is hurting your chances of getting dates.

1. a. Would you do say nothing and hope for the best?

    b. Would you explain your concern and stop hanging around your friend?

    c. Would you distance yourself from your friend and hope he or she doesn't notice?

    d. Would you do something else? What would you do?

2. What if you sense that your other friends are starting to distance themselves from both of you. Neither of you get as many invites or calls to group events. Would this change what you would do? Explain why.

3. What if you are your friend's only friend? Would this change what you would do? Explain why.

4. What if your friend confessed that he or she is embarrassed by the weight but cannot lose the weight in spite of several diets and exercise? Would this change what you would do? Explain why.

5. What if your friend asks you before you do anything if his or her weight embarrasses you? Would this change what you would do? Explain why.

PROBLEM 16

Suppose you are asked to write a six-page paper. You wait until the night before the assignment is due to write the paper. The same evening there is a sold-out concert that you really wanted to attend. A friend stops by with an extra ticket and asks you if you'd like to use it. When told about the paper you need to write, your friend offers to give you a paper written two years ago in a similar assignment but for a different teacher.

1.　　a.　Would you refuse the offer of the paper?

　　　b.　Would you accept the offer of the paper?

　　　c.　Would you accept the offer of the paper but make a few quick changes to it?

　　　d.　Would you do something else? What would you do?

2.　What if your friend's paper received a "C," but you usually get "B's"? Would this change what you would do? Explain why.

3.　What if your friend's paper received an "A," and you think using this paper will get you a higher grade than writing one of your own? Would this change what you would do? Explain why.

4.　What if your friend offers to sell you the paper? Would this change what you would do? Explain why.

5.　What if you feel you will learn little or nothing by writing the paper on your own? Would this change what you would do? Explain why.

PROBLEM 17

Suppose a friend appears to be very upset. When you ask her what's wrong, she agrees to tell you only if you swear not to tell anyone. She confides to you that she has been molested by one of her parents.

1.   a.   Would you honor your word and not tell anyone?

        b.   Would you break your word and tell someone about it?

        c.   Would you suggest that she tell her other parent, if she has not done so already?

        d.   Would you do something else? What would you do?

2.   What if your friend is male? Would this change what you would do? Explain why.

3.   What if your friend tells you her parents have been having marital problems, so she is afraid that telling them what happened could end their marriage? Would this change what you would do? Explain why.

4.   What if your friend tells you that she has told her other parent what happened, and that parent has told her not to tell anyone? Would this change what you would do? Explain why.

5.   What if your friend tells you that she has told her other parent, but that parent does not believe her? Would this change what you would do? Explain why.

6.   What if your friend has a tendency to exaggerate on some occasions? Would this change what you would do? Explain why.

7.   What if your friend tells you the abusive parent has apologized? Would this change what you would do? Explain why.

8.   What if you keep your word not to tell, but after several weeks you see your friend is becoming increasingly upset? Would this change what you would do? Explain why.

PROBLEM 18

Suppose a student in one of your classes complains to the teacher that it is hard for him to complete his classwork because you and your best friend are talking. Since the two of you have been warned before about talking in class, the teacher kicks both of you out of the class for the day. From that day forward, your friend begins teasing the student about his looks and asks some bigger students to "teach this guy a lesson." When confronted, the student asks everyone to leave him alone, but your friend shows no sign of letting up.

1. a. Would you do nothing since the student started the trouble and this is between him and your best friend?

　　b. Would you ask the student to apologize for getting the two of you in trouble in hopes that the apology would end the bullying?

　　c. Would you tell your friend that he is getting carried away with his revenge and that he must stop if you are to remain friends?

　　d. Would you do something else? What would you do?

2. What if this student had gotten other students in trouble by reporting bad behavior? Would this change what you would do? Explain why.

3. What if your best friend confided to you that it was never his or her intention to have the student physically hurt, but rather to merely teach him a lesson? Would this change what you would do? Explain why.

4. What if your best friend got in a lot of trouble at home after being kicked out of the class? Would this change what you would do? Explain why.

5. What if the student asked you for help and told you that he had admitted to your friend that he "regrets reporting both of you to the teacher." Would this change what you would do? Explain why.

PROBLEM 19

Suppose a friend of yours is constantly bragging.

1.   a.   Would you tell your friend how you feel about his or her bragging?
           If so, how would you tell your friend?

      b.   Would you try to ignore the bragging?

      c.   Would you do something else? What would you do?

2.   What if the bragging is limited to one ability? Would this change what you
     would do? Explain why.

3.   What if your friend's bragging is completely baseless? Would this change what
     you would do? Explain why.

4.   What if your friend is truly talented, so the bragging is factual? Would this
     change what you would do? Explain why.

5.   What if your friend does not have a lot of friends, and you believe the bragging
     is an attempt to get more attention from people? Would this change what you
     would do? Explain why.

6.   What if your friend is bragging about an ability in a field in which you perform
     even better than he or she? Would this change what you would do?
     Explain why.

7.   What if your friend is bragging about an ability in a field in which you do poorly?
     Would that change what you would do? Explain why.

PROBLEM 20

Suppose your cell phone was stolen from your locker. You discover the cell phone was stolen by the best performing member of your school's basketball team. This year's team has a good chance to compete for the state championship. If you report the theft, you know the team member will be removed from the team.

1.
   a. Would you report the theft?

   b. Would you wait and report the theft after the season?

   c. Would you do something else? What would you do?

2. What if your school is very small and an opportunity to go to the state finals may never come again? Would this change what you would do? Explain why.

3. What if you want to try out for the basketball team next year? Would this change what you would do? Explain why.

4. What if the team member returns the cell phone to your locker but never speaks to you about the theft? Would this change what you would do? Explain why.

5. What if the team member returns the cell phone to you and apologizes, but the phone has a new scratch on the screen? Would this change what you would do? Explain why.

6. What if you approach the team member, who denies stealing the cell phone, and the other members of the team plead with you not to report the theft? Would this change what you would do? Explain why.

7. What if the other members on the team offer to buy you a new cell phone? Would this change what you would do? Explain why.

PROBLEM 21

Suppose someone asks you out on a date but does not mention anything about who is paying for the date.

1.   a.   Would you assume that the costs of the date will be split equally?

       b.   Would you assume that whomever asked you out would pay for the date?

       c.   Would you do something else? What would you do?

2.   What if this person asks you out on the condition that the costs of the date be split equally? Would this change what you would do? Explain why.

3.   What if you have wanted to date this person for a long time? Would this change what you would do? Explain why.

4.   What if you think this person does not have much money? Would this change what you would do? Explain why.

5.   What if the date is going to be very expensive? Would this change what you would do? Explain why.

6.   What if the date is going to be very inexpensive? Would this change what you would do? Explain why.

7.   What if you plan to ask someone out on a date? When would you discuss who pays for what? Explain why.

PROBLEM 22

Suppose you are told you have an incurable disease and within a month you will lapse into an irreversible coma and never regain consciousness. The doctor tells you that the hospital would provide supportive care and could, if necessary, maintain your bodily functions using life-support machines. She also tells you that you are able to determine your own treatment through written instructions to your doctors.

1. a. Would you have the hospital maintain your bodily functions, hoping that either science will find a cure or you will make a miraculous recovery?

    b. Would you direct your doctor through written instructions to remove any life-support machines and/or discontinue nutritional support if it was clear that you were in a persistent vegetative state (no awareness of your self or your environment, no ability to think or feel emotions) and would never recover?

    c. Would you leave the decision up to family members (if there are any)?

    d. Would you do something else? What would you do?

2. What if the cost of your illness is totally covered by medical insurance? Would this change what you would do? Explain why.

3. What if the cost of maintaining your bodily functions would have to be paid by your family? Would this change what you would do? Explain why.

4. What if the medical resources needed to sustain your life could be used to save other patients who might recover and go on to lead normal lives? Would this change what you would do? Explain why.

5. What if you know that every year you wait for a cure, you will incur more brain damage? Would this change what you would do? Explain why.

PROBLEM 23

Suppose a school friend you enjoy being around tells you about a political philosophy in which he or she believes. You consider it extremist and the complete opposite of your own philosophy.

1.   a.   Would you end the friendship?

     b.   Would you ignore your political differences and maintain the friendship?

     c.   Would you tell your friend of your different belief and then try to make a pact to avoid the subject in the future?

     d.   Would you try to convince your friend that his or her belief is "wrong?"

     e.   Would you do something else? What would you do?

2.   What if your friend's philosophy calls for violent solutions to what he or she perceives as injustice? Would this change what you would do? Explain why.

3.   What if your friend's philosophy calls for very vocal and active nonviolent demonstrations of his or her beliefs around your other friends in school? Would this change what you would do? Explain why.

4.   What if your friend's philosophy would result in greater justice for the poor through whatever means are necessary? Would this change what you would do? Explain why.

PROBLEM 24

Suppose you find a paper bag containing $40,000 in unmarked bills hidden among some weeds in a city parking lot. No one is aware of your find.

1.   a.   Would you keep the cash for yourself and tell no one?

       b.   Would you report your find to the police?

       c.   Would you tell no one and wait to see if anyone reports losing the money?

       d.   Would you do something else? What would you do?

2.   What if the money is reported lost by a person who refuses to answer police questions about where it came from and what it is to be used for? Would this change what you would do? Explain why.

3.   What if you suspect the money was lost or abandoned by drug dealers? Would this change what you would do? Explain why.

4.   What if you suspect the money is from a bank robbery? Would this change what you would do? Explain why.

5.   What if the money was stolen from a large, multinational corporation? Would this change what you would do? Explain why.

6.   What if the money was stolen from a very large labor union? Would this change what you would do? Explain why.

7.   What if the money was stolen from a successful law firm? Would this change what you would do? Explain why.

PROBLEM 25

Suppose you and your best friend are in an automobile accident while you are driving. The two of you had been drinking at a party, and you caused the accident. Your best friend is paralyzed from the waist down as a result. His or her family and some of your classmates blame you for your friend's paralysis.

1. a. Would you accept responsibility for what happened to your friend?

    b. Would you not accept responsibility for what happened to your friend?

    c. Would you accept your part in causing the accident but not feel responsible for your friend's paralysis?

    d. Would you accept/feel something else? Explain what.

2. What if your friend, obviously upset about the paralysis, tells you that you are to blame for what happened? Would this change what you would do? Explain why.

3. What if it was your friend's idea to get a ride home from the party with you? Would this change what you would do? Explain why.

4. What if the accident was not your fault, but witnesses said you were slow to react to the other vehicle? Would this change what you would do? Explain why.

5. What if someone at the party had tried to tell you that you were not in any condition to drive? Would this change what you would do? Explain why.

6. What if the parents of your injured friend ask you to spend one night every weekend helping to care for your friend until you finish high school? Would you be willing to do this? Do you think such a request would be fair?

PROBLEM 26

Suppose you apply for a summer job running a forklift. One of the questions on the job application asks if you have ever used illegal drugs. The question requires you to mark a "Yes" or "No" box. Suppose you smoked marijuana twice in the last year with a friend who had some, but you have never bought any and don't plan to buy any.

1. a. Would you answer the question "Yes"?

    b. Would you answer the question "No"?

    c. Would you skip the question?

    d. Would you do something else? What would you do?

2. What if the job you want is with the company your mother or father works for? Would this change what you would do? Explain why.

3. What if the application process concludes with a polygraph (lie detector) test in which you are asked if you have answered all questions on the application truthfully? Would this change what you would do? Explain why.

4. What if the job is with the local police force? Would this change what you would do? Explain why.

5. What if the job is with a religious organization of which you are a member? Would this change what you would do? Explain why.

6. What if the company policy states that no one can be hired who has ever willingly used an illegal drug? Do you feel this is an acceptable policy? Explain why.

7. What if you have never smoked marijuana but drank alcohol illegally a year ago? How would you answer the question? Explain why.

8. Do you feel such a question is a fair question to ask on a job application? Explain why.

PROBLEM 27

Suppose one night you are out with a group of friends. Another group of people starts throwing verbal insults at your group. Suddenly a fight breaks out between your group and the other group. The other group wins the fight, but some of them continue to assault three of your friends who had been knocked to the ground while none of the others try to stop them. As a result, one of your friends suffers permanent paralysis, and the other two are seriously injured.

1.   a.   Do you feel all the people in the other group should be prosecuted equally for the injuries to your friends? If so, explain why.

       b.   Do you feel only those few people in the group who continued to beat your friends on the ground should be prosecuted for the injuries? If so, explain why.

       c.   Do you suggest something else? If so, explain.

2.   What if your group had started the verbal insults? Would this change who should be prosecuted? Explain why.

3.   What if one person from the other group only engaged in verbal insults and did not engage in any violence? Should this person be prosecuted? Explain why.

4.   Should the person who made the first verbal gibe bear more responsibility than the others? Explain why or why not.

5.   Should the person who threw the first blow bear more responsibility than the others? Explain why or why not.

PROBLEM 28

Suppose you are out with a group of male friends. Some are good friends and some are acquaintances. The group runs into three girls you all know. They invite you over to one of the girls' houses knowing her parents won't be there. You put on some music and continue to party with your friends. You and two of your friends are talking with one of the girls in the living room when you hear a commotion in the back of the house. You look into one of the rooms and see two of your friends holding down a struggling, hysterical girl while another is trying to remove her clothes.

1.   a.   Would you try to stop the assault?

         b.   Would you consider it unfortunate but none of your business because you are not personally involved in the assault?

         c.   Would you join the assault?

         d.   Would you do something else? What would you do?

2. What if the girl had willingly gone into the room with your two friends? Would this change what you would do? Explain why.

3. What if you know the girl involved has a reputation for being sexually promiscuous? Would this change what you would do? Explain why.

4. What if one of the boys involved is your best friend? Would this change what you would do? Explain why.

5. What if the two boys told you that the girl had invited them into the room and to mind your own business? Would this change what you would do? Explain why.

PROBLEM 29

1. Select ten qualities from the list below that you think are the most important for someone your age to possess. Number them 1 - 10, with 1 being the most important. Then explain why each is important to you.

_____ funny	_____ has style and class
_____ attractive	_____ a good brother or sister
_____ tough	_____ honest and fair
_____ popular	_____ friendly
_____ tall	_____ considerate
_____ kind	_____ reliable
_____ intelligent	_____ good listener
_____ athletic	_____ patient

2. Select ten qualities from the list below that you think are the most important for a friend to possess. Number them 1 - 10, with 1 being the most important. If the ten qualities you selected for question #2 are different from the ten qualities you selected for question #1, explain why there is a difference.

_____ funny	_____ has style and class
_____ attractive	_____ honest and fair
_____ tough	_____ friendly
_____ popular	_____ positive thinker
_____ loyal	_____ considerate
_____ kind	_____ reliable
_____ intelligent	_____ good listener
_____ athletic	_____ patient

3. Select ten qualities from the list below that you value most in someone with whom you would share a romantic relationship. Number them 1 - 10, with 1 being the most important. If those ten qualities are different from the ones you selected in the previous two lists, explain why.

_____ funny	_____ has style and class
_____ attractive	_____ honest and fair
_____ tough	_____ friendly
_____ popular	_____ positive thinker
_____ loyal	_____ considerate
_____ kind	_____ reliable
_____ intelligent	_____ good listener
_____ athletic	_____ patient

4. Select ten qualities from the list below which you think are the most important for a parent to possess. Number them 1 - 10, with 1 being the most important. Explain why these qualities are important to you.

_____ funny	_____ has style and class
_____ attractive	_____ good parent
_____ tough	_____ honest and fair
_____ popular	_____ friendly
_____ tall	_____ affluent
_____ kind	_____ has a good job
_____ intelligent	_____ considerate
_____ athletic	_____ reliable
_____ good listener	_____ patient

5. From the list below, select any qualities you believe you do not possess. If you select more than one, number them with 1 being the most important. Which quality or qualities would you like most to develop? Explain why these qualities are important for you to have.

_____ funny	_____ has style and class
_____ attractive	_____ honest and fair
_____ tough	_____ friendly
_____ popular	_____ affluent
_____ loving	_____ has a good job
_____ kind	_____ positive thinker
_____ intelligent	_____ considerate
_____ athletic	_____ reliable
_____ good listener	_____ patient